WATER
I WON'T
TOUCH

ALSO BY KAYLEB RAE CANDRILLI

All the Gay Saints
What Runs Over

WATER
I WON'T
TOUCH

KAYLEB RAE CANDRILLI

COPPER CANYON PRESS

PORT TOWNSEND, WASHINGTON

Cover art: Stephan Zirwes, Leo Sprungturm2_12C1185.jpg, 2016,
fine-art print, 30 × 40 cm.

Copper Canyon Press is in residence at Fort Worden State Park
in Port Townsend, Washington, under the auspices of Centrum.
Centrum is a gathering place for artists and creative thinkers
from around the world, students of all ages and backgrounds,
and audiences seeking extraordinary cultural enrichment.

Library of Congress Cataloging-in-Publication Data
Names: Candrilli, Kayleb Rae, author.
Title: Water I won't touch / Kayleb Rae Candrilli.
Other titles: Water I will not touch
Description: Port Townsend, Washington : Copper Canyon Press, [2021] |
Summary: "A collection of poems by Kayleb Rae Candrilli"—Provided by
publisher.
Identifiers: LCCN 2020047953 | ISBN 9781556596179 (paperback)
Subjects: LCGFT: Poetry.
Classification: LCC PS3603.A5374 W38 2021 | DDC 811/.6—dc23
LC record available at https://lccn.loc.gov/2020047953

98765432 FIRST PRINTING

COPPER CANYON PRESS

Post Office Box 271
Port Townsend, Washington 98368
www.coppercanyonpress.org

again, and always, for jack

It's only water, it's only fire, it's only love.

ODESZA & Zyra

CONTENTS

WATER
I WON'T
TOUCH

SAND & SILT

In the beginning, there was a boy
who touched me as he shouldn't have.

His hands around my ankles—claustrophobic—
a plot of cattails on the water's black silt.

We all have a story like this,
innocent in its setting, nefarious

how it stays spurred into our bones
as we grow.

I think I knew I was a boy
when the boy touched me.

I know this boy is now
a violent man

with a large collection of semi-
automatic rifles. Some things

are so absolute. The point
at which rain becomes snow. The way

fruit eventually spoils
even under unblemished skin.

If I make a metaphor of my body,
it's a desert. One part longing,

one part need, the rest withstanding. Of course
I would prefer to be thirsty

for nothing. I'd rather do so much
than be touched in this angry dark.

Violent men want me to be a violent man.
Or they want me dead.

What a privilege to have an option.

ONE GEOGRAPHY OF BELONGING

After Ocean Vuong

What becomes of the girl
no longer a girl? Dearest Mother,

the stretch marks from my once-breasts
have migrated

to their new tectonic flats.
But you can always find hints

of what used to be. Trust me,
it is more beautiful

this way, to look closely
at my body and name it things like:

    Pangaea & history & so, so warm.

Look at me now
and see how blood

faithfully takes the shape
of its body,

never asking
too many questions.

Dearest Mother, how many rivers
did I run across your belly?

Do you love
that they will never dry up?

Mother, I'll make all
this water worth it.

ON THE WAYS OUR MOUTHS BETRAY US

In Pennsylvania there is a puddle of quicksand
that only swallows slowly. This is how I once enjoyed
being eaten: whole, deliberately, a thrashing woodland

spectacle. When I was young, I tied cherry stems
with my tongue because I wanted my mouth
practiced before knots could be demanded of it.

When I was young, I ate all the birds the sky
made available. Haven't we all chewed
through something tough and survived?

    :::

Years ago my mother asked
if I was trans. I said no.

We were in the car, in a parking lot,
outside a Barnes & Noble, eating Panera,

and I said no when I meant
Yes, yes of course.

WATER I WON'T TOUCH

It's hard to explain my persistent
sadness when I keep so many

blueberries frozen in the freezer.
Nirvana, in the past, was plenty

of fruit, and all the moments spent outside
of myself. But currently, I am trying to pull

the planets from retrograde and remember
all the ways my drinking can kill me.

I still want a lake-sized sip. This is such
a citrus habit of mine, such acid rusting

away my tooth enamel. I never learned
to drive because I knew one day

I would learn to drink. I have always
been almost selfless like this. Sure,

there are some things I regret:
I once left my mother's Minolta

on the hood of a car, and I regret
each memory lost in turn.

Because I am an alcoholic,
my memories are seven amens

and a few holy spirits from
hog-tied. I name all my favorite

bars after churches. Pigeons are
swans if you squint. You know,

the cherry blossoms bloomed again
this year, despite all the damage

to my liver. And autumn is coming,
even though I've said things

I do not mean.

ON THE ABUSE OF SLEEP AIDS

back when my mother shared

a bed with my father, she took

three benadryl every night. she said:

i thought he was going to kill me.

and for years, we stayed drowsy

together, lulled by that incessant

rhythm of violence. i took

to speaking exclusively with the dirt

beneath our home. i asked it so

politely to invite the whole house

into the earth and keep it there.

SOME THOUGHTS ON LUCK

:::

superstitious sicilians in the mountains—
all we spoke about

was mickey mantle and my father's
old mafia ties.

can you imagine
the rabbits' feet hung

round my neck during hunting
season, the fur

matted and the nails
so desperate

to finally decompose.
what does it mean

to carry a dead
animal so close to your heart

in hopes you might
kill some more.

:::

:::

when i learned to swallow
i began to drink

the ocean. so much booze
it might as well

have been sea salt. i was drunk,
in a bad love, and stevie nicks

was my only god.
what is god

besides a superstition,
belief in that

which will never be proved.
my inner thigh

is tattooed with
a rock star—

so holy, but still proving
the way liquor can take

hold of even your skin,
make it

something you've never seen before
and will see every day after.

:::

:::

my father has always hated
women, though

he has always needed them.
what a rich history,

this narrative of misogyny.
counting fist-falls

as sheep
is a storied simile.

finally, i am no longer drunk
or superstitious.

and though i am marked
by having been so,

i can feel love now,
like my father never has.

i am thankful to have been born
his daughter

because if i had been born my father's son,
forget about it.

:::

ON THE BENEFITS OF LEARNING BY EXAMPLE

I'm always writing about heavy things: headstones,
fathers, a feather painted with blood. Below the equator,

bats are boiling in the night sky. I know this is the product
of global heat, humans, but all I remember is my father

taking bat after bat from the night sky with a BB gun.
The first thing I ever learned is that it's not hard

to kill. He held them together,
dead in his hands and rolling like tiny red plums.

When I fall in love with my partner it's as fast
as a downed bird, smooth and in

                                a tailspin.

Our bodies are not meant to live
together in such queer, bloodred

harmony. But some sins are sweeter than others.
Sodom and Grace are all wrapped up

in the backwoods and yes, I will always be loving
my partner just like this—soft

and dusted in Pennsylvania dirt. As far
as I walk from my roots, they grow to reach—

and that teaches me everything
I need to know about being good.

SESTINA WRITTEN AS THOUGH GENESIS

I.

The Christmas lights are gorgeous around your wrists
until your wrists are burning. Most things are like this, beautiful
until they are no longer beautiful—gunmetal before it's a gun,
volcano before it's an evacuation. One man's kill is another man's
dinner if he is desperate and hungry. The world is ruthless. It's moonrise
again. And of course, I've held a gun in one hand, dead animal in the other.

II.

I've buckshot through an aorta and regretted it. I'm from just another
American valley dense with opioid smoke. Yes, I've checked the wrists
of my father doped well into the sky—his eyes white as clouds lit by moonrise.
Yes, I've tried to exorcise my roots from the Pennsylvania thicket. But it's beautiful
that I'm still all bramble and picker bushes. You know how it goes, every man
around here has bragged about severing a snake's body from its head, and about his guns.

III.

Not much survives in rural America. Though it wants to. My father buried some guns in the hillside, and I'm sure he'll be back. The reflection of a window in a window is another opportunity for escape. When I was young, I climbed trees for vantage and watched as men pulled wind from the air and left empty promises. Honestly, all the hope I kept in my wrists must have worked just as well as blood, because I'm still warm-bodied and beautiful.

Now, I doctor the thunder in Photoshop and just like that the storm is half over. It's moonrise.

IV.

And yes, when I speak about my partner it is hyperbole, the pigs flying over a rising moon,
the unicorns entering the horse race. And it is all true. When I met my partner, I took the gun
I kept in my body out of my body, and I have never felt lighter or less full of metal. How beautiful
that we sang our first duet in a swamp. My partner confused an alligator for *just another*
basilisk and I asked them to marry me. Photosynthesize me for the next century. Kiss my wrists
until they clot. My partner recognizes my boot print in snow, and we are always teaching men.

22

v.

Something about love. Something about union and compromise. I want to invite all American men to our wedding. Someplace where water meets sand with its arms open. We'll marry at night, the moon risen and reflecting the sun's blushed skin. We will size our ring fingers and tie the silk of silkworms around our wrists, which will stay tied for as many decades as we can muster. Bring your Pop Rocks and know the love that's begun. When my partner says *sauna, sauna,* I know that means *soon, soon.* Every day, I show my mother this love in my cupped hands. I tell her, *Now, even the chipped paint on the windowsill is beautiful.*

VI.

The worst of my life is the rust I grow in the nail clipper, what a blessing that is. Humans want to be full of anything at all. And it might as well be affection, dandelions, or letting the boat take you, unmanned, to float wherever you're headed. All gold is an echo of your feet on the ground. Who were you in another life? Do you remember? I have spent all my lives waiting for an unmade bed, cross-breezes, and this particular sunrise. There are no wolves left to cry wolf in my bed. I hear the music of the leaves. Finally, the god I pray to has begun to record-spin on the weekends. God drops the needle and of course it's house music, each beat finding its way to my wrists.

VII.

When I was young, I would watch my mother split firewood, the only warmth in all that snow. Beautiful is a mother's love for her child in a parking lot—hand tight around a wrist. One day soon, all that humans know will be the heat of the atmosphere, desperate love, and the relief of the moon rising. We know what we've begun.

◇◇◇

WATER I WON'T TOUCH

My partner & I only believe
in good omens,

because we are young and gay
and generally unbothered

when god tells us
we are misbehaved.

In response, we invite hell-
hounds into our bed

and invest in a proper vacuum.
Religion in America

is taken much
too seriously. And though

we are dying,
please watch us rejoice

simply at not having killed
the houseplants, simply

at having cooked a meal
even and through.

SUMMERING IN WILDWOOD, NJ

in a few days, i'll be on a beach
so bright i can see the sun through my fingers,

each thin vein lit
up blue like a heron's leg.

this poem is not so much about a beach
as it is about arriving,

blowing stop signs
until the coast affirms

that lines are always changing,
and the tide tells me

my body can morph
as many times as it needs.

ON CRESCENTS & WANING

Just before anesthesia
took me

to the bottom of the ocean,
I looked down my hospital gown

and admired, for the last time,
the fullness of this original body.

My original body had many marvels
but I always wished it for

someone else—spent
years daydreaming of my body

neatly disassembled and sent
to more deserving homes.

But one cannot give oneself
away quite like this.

After the scalpel, my breast tissue
became biological waste.

My body shrunk
to its new original.

Now, under all this
almost-newness,

I watch my own heart as it beats.
I look at my life more

closely than ever, and how beautiful
it is, just under the skin,

alive & alive & alive—
like a warm moon.

ON TRAVELING TOGETHER

In a Super 8 just outside Iowa
City, two twelve-year-old boys

cuddle on the lobby couch,
scrolling on their phones.

It's four in the morning, and they don't expect
me, or anyone,

in this holy space they've drawn
for themselves.

Their parents are asleep
on the third floor, resting

before a hockey tournament or some other
rough-and-tumble game.

It's clear by the way the boys
jump as I walk by:

their parents know nothing.
The floor is lava.

The continental
breakfast will start soon.

The couch they're on is an island
I've been to.

WE REMAIN FOOLISHLY HOPEFUL
(OR, OBITUARY FOR THE TOPSOIL)

I am forever concerned

for the quality of the breast milk

I'll never make. My partner and I are out

here in the sun, gardening in our ugly human suits

and lusting the next produce. We take the temperature

of each bell pepper, each tomato, and we hope for a healthy

harvest. We are always hoping for the best. But humans

have sent all their worst inventions straight into

the soil. You can taste the plastic before

it's even grown, before it's even

melting in your mouth.

ON HAVING FORGOTTEN TO RECYCLE

The Arctic is a wetland

and the Dead Sea is dying, too. The chapped

lips of salt have begun to peel back, a tide in constant

surrender. Humans amaze me with their knack to kill, again

and again, so endlessly. Though I am concerned for the earth's rapid

erosion, I have done it to myself. I have cleaved whole mountains from

my chest and sent them to soak in an offshore landfill. My breasts, I imagine,

are long dead, floating alongside jellyfish and plastic straws. I feel surprised

by this new smallness—this body postanesthesia, post disposing all

the flesh I just didn't want anymore. The world is growing

warmer. And it is true; I am smaller now, with a heart

that much closer to the sun.

ECHO

When they look inside
your chest, the sonogram calls

your heart an orchid, each
petal pulpy and abnormally

palpitating. You and I
both imagined it would

behave this way, flowering
too big where it shouldn't.

We have both pressed
our ears to conch shells

and clocked your heart
as it gallops

into another season,
another faulty

bloom. Perhaps it is an early
symptom of aging, to worry

like this, with every sense,
in every room of our bodies.

Perhaps it is wrong of me
to be so critical

of your heart—to want it
to speak more like mine.

MY PARTNER WANTS ME TO WRITE THEM
A POEM ABOUT DREW BARRYMORE

and, of course, this poem has to be about home and longing for it.
There is a moment in most people's days when we remember

both the vastness of the universe and our father's opioid addiction.
Of course, I've made the decision to call 911, but I've also hung up

the phone to fetch a cool bucket of water and let it rain down.
Yes, aliens most surely exist, but what about rehab and therapy

and enough resources to go around, right here on Earth. I am tired
and I'm sure you are too. It's true that not everyone can be saved

but that doesn't mean you should keep your hands in your pockets,
thumbing lint and that single bicentennial quarter you've smoothed

with wishing. When my partner saw the Grand Canyon for the first
time, they wept. The whole sky was the same color, a massive,

unimaginable thing. Bless the sun who keeps us alive and full
of our wonder and warm blood. Bless the son whose mother tries

to keep him alive and warm as the shakes take over. I once split
open a live lizard and found maggots. It's true that we can hold

just about everything inside us, whether we want to or not.
If I had any freedom at all, I'd take out my partner's ovarian cysts

and fertilize a garden, but what do I know about love, or about
soil, besides how they both feel just the same in my mouth.

VALENTINE, NEBRASKA: CHERRY COUNTY

:::

My boxers are often ill-fitting
because my thighs

span so much
of the Appalachian Trail.

My partner loves my body
without hesitation.

To be honest, this body
could probably use some

more modification
but won't get any

more than it's already gotten.
From here on out, I will take up

the same amount of space
in Appalachia as in

the hypothetical heart
of the sand hills.

Impermanent and already decomposing,
our bodies are just

stardust this,
stardust that.

:::

:::

Once, long before we met,
my partner asked a butcher

for work. And was told,
Meat is a family business.

When I was a kid
animals were unzipped in my kitchen,

naked and blood-raw,
strewn on black trash bags—

all those hind legs disassembled
and vacuum-packed

                        for colder days.

And I think what a perfect
family this will be,

me and my partner:
so red, and constantly sharpened.

:::

:::

Just before my double mastectomy
my partner asked whether the surgeon would open

me deep enough to see
my heart. And though

my ribcage was left
in its original arches,

I imagine a knife blade
is what has come closest to my core—

a violent scraping of breast
tissue from muscle

that still aches
months and months later.

:::

:::

This Valentine's Day, we spin
another allusion

toward anatomical hearts,
and all I can conjure

is my partner's latest
echocardiogram,   bumpy
                         and upside down.

We love each other so much
we are trying to keep

this life going
despite all our simultaneous body—

all this ridiculous flesh.

:::

YOU'VE HEARD THIS BEFORE:
THE ONLY WAY OUT IS THROUGH

When my family burnt it all, we

even burnt the dolls. I write

about this all the time, but have you

ever seen anything like it? A pit

of ashes and dozens of porcelain

hands, sprouting up like girlish

weeds. So far in this life, I have

heard a number of unacceptable

apologies and they have all begun

with *I'm sorry* and ended with

OxyContin. It's a shame

the Pennsylvanian landscape

is just waterfalls, coal, and

pharmaceutical drugs. I wish

there were more libraries and less

violence, but I have always been so

painfully hopeful. On Facebook,

my sibling's boyfriend

messages, *they've abandoned me*

at the airport, I don't know what

to do and I resist the urge to tell

him: that's what they do to all

of us. Instead I write back,

Oh no! There are so many ways

to be angry at just one thing.

I haven't seen my sibling in nine years

and sometimes I have a temper

with my hand fruit, bite it a little

too hard, because chewing

is such a frustrated act

to begin with. When I was seven

my father said he was going

to push me all the way around

on the swing set; I leapt

off at the peak, airborne

and so sure of his strength.

Centripetal or centrifugal, neither

matters if your face meets the ground,

alive with blood and mulch.

When I was eleven, my father told me

the legend of Pope Joan, and I loved

how she hid her her-ness in plain

sight. So invisibly woman. She

gave birth, was put to death—and I

imagined she must have been raped.

She must have. I believe that

had I known one trans person

as a child, I'd have half as many scars

as an adult. I could have come

around to this body so much sooner

and without as many cigarette burns,

my whole body a cratered and earthbound moon. Often, when I am drunk

and alone, white men ask me

what I have against white men

if I want to look like one, and then

they follow me all the way home.

It seems every man in America

has been taught to stalk real quiet

in a forest of dry leaves. Myself included.

I am not a man, nor do I desire to be,

but I suppose I have always been

a hunter, armed and unwilling

to consider my own shortcomings.

After I woke from my double

mastectomy, I thought about the day

my father killed two doe with one bullet

and we butchered them both, right

there and then. There are two

of everything worth having two of.

Now I am so visibly trans, I am being

photographed in white light, my scars

lit like dogwood crowns. It's hard

to know what to make of this, when

all I have ever known is blood-

red and a wilderness. Recently

a new cloud was introduced

to the atlas, known for its apocalypse

lip color, its mouth opening dark-deep—

like a sinkhole, or your trans lover's eager

and previously abused mouth. Nobody

wants to be lonely, least of all me.

Maybe I am interested in clouds

because I am one, stratus sliced post-

surgery, or maybe it's because I'm an air

sign and have been missing my family

for years, despite all their lava,

all their hot, angry fuel. My mother

is a better whistler than me, but

I think we both understand air,

and our mouths, and the best

ways to call for help. Listen,

there is a razor in the apple

and the apple is the earth. Listen,

my nightmares are dreams in which

everyone walks the same direction—

that rhythmic lockstep. Both of my

grandmothers considered abortion.

Can you imagine?

Being so close to nothing.

◇◇◇

I CHALLENGE MY FATHER TO AN ARM-WRESTLING COMPETITION AND FINALLY WIN

//

More than a decade has passed since I saw my father,
in the parking lot of a Wilkes-Barre strip mall. More than

a decade since he took my sibling to the Hawaiian Islands
and dosed them with oxy, meth, and heroin. In that order.

None of this should have surprised me. But, of course, it did.
When my sibling finally came back, they brought home blown

veins, a back full of scars, and a pillowcase full of bruises.
My father once forced a crack pipe into my hands, right after

I was discharged from the hospital, and right after
my eighteenth birthday. I'm sure there's something beautiful

to say, somewhere, tucked between the facts
of our lives and my old Pokémon collection.

My sibling is sober and vibrant and alive.
My sibling is way more fun than I've ever been.

Nothing should surprise me,
but it does, and that's enough.

//

//

I have so few fond memories of my father,
but what I have, I hold.

He read me the entire *Kamandi* comic series,
and I studied *The Last Boy on Earth*.

I learned how to survive an apocalypse
and how to be a boy.

It's 2020 now, and both are proving useful.
When I was seven years old,

my father and I play-fought with inflatable
circus swords in the sunroom.

When his sword came down, I expected a knighting,
but instead, the plastic seam

sliced my cornea. I suppose most children
taste this same bittersweet

syrup when they think about their fathers:
sugar dressing up a lemon,

an eye patch over a rivulet, a pretend pirate
only until the wound heals.

//

//

When the stock market crashes, I am happy
to have invested in nothing but hot fries and orzo.
Sometimes it is easy to have so little,

or at least uncomplicated. My mother loved hip-hop
and my father beat her for it. If she and I drove around
alone, she'd turn up the radio and explain: *It's like*

the more money we come across the more problems we see.
My mother had our property logged of all its timber
so I could move away and learn to write poetry.

My father spent all that maple money on marriage
counseling, but my mother wasn't in attendance.
Sometimes I want to go back, just for a meal

of Steak-umms and frozen orange juice.
But who has the time to rewind. Those downed
trees I used to climb are sawdust.

//

WATER WE WON'T TOUCH

Reunited after years apart,

my sibling is how I imagined

they would be, hair pink

and lit up like a highway flare—

a fire that always tries

to keep itself alive, even

in the rain, or as the tide rolls up.

For years my father had my sibling

water-locked, drug-spun—

surrounded by the Pacific

and saline-flushed needles.

And still my sibling burned.

When we were young,

my father used his hands

for everything. He used his hands

to describe how lightning

almost took him. He

and the lightning

the only bodies on the beach.

His feet smoked up, charred

on the bottoms, a spider-

web of fire spun as the storm

lashed onto shore. The sand

turned to silica glass around him.

My father has always been spared

and my father is the closest thing I know

to a sinner. What is the third degree

if not a near smiting?

Sometimes, I wonder

about the vastness of the ocean,

and how best to avoid its anger.

My sibling and I loved each other

most during storms. I know this.

When my sibling tells me—

after all these years—about

the pink lightning that hovered

over a town full of pink houses, I know

that we haven't been totally beaten.

What is a family if not preparation?

We can smell a storm coming

before anyone. I swear

we can taste it rolling in.

MY PARTNER WANTS ME TO WRITE THEM
A POEM ABOUT SHERYL CROW

but all I want to do is marry them on a beach

that refuses to take itself too seriously.

So much of our lives have been serious.

Over time, I've learned that love is most astonishing

when it persists after learning where we come from.

When I bring my partner to my childhood home

it is all bullets and needles and trash bags held

at arm's length. It is my estranged father's damp

bed of cardboard and cigar boxes filled

with gauze and tarnished spoons. It is hard

to clean a home, but it is harder to clean

the memory of it. When I was young, my

father would light lavender candles and shoot

up. Now, my partner and I light a fire that will

burn all traces of the family that lived here.

Black plastic smoke curdles up, and loose bullets

discharge in the flames. My partner holds

my hand as gunfire rings through

the birch trees. Though this is almost

beautiful, it is not. And while I'm being honest:

My partner and I spend most of our time

on Earth feeding one another citrus fruits

and enough strength to go on. Every morning

I pack them half a grapefruit and some sugar.

And they tell me it's just sweet enough.

HERE WE ARE, AGING TOGETHER,
JUST LIKE WE SAID WE WOULD

For your birthday, we pretend
prehistoric. I fill our apartment

with inflatable dinosaurs, scaly ice
cream cake, and raw meat.

You have always wanted
a birthday just like this:

carbon-dated back
to before humans

decided to chew
all sorts of things. We play pretend

so well you can barely smell the plastic,
or remember anything about outside

and the blood moon that hangs,
wanting to become

a whole new animal
in your eyes.

When I eroded the landscape
of my body,

you drew a fresh map,
topographical and understanding.

When my blood was outside
my body you kept

the carnivores at bay.
This is what we've promised

one another, to try and live
and live and live

until the earth caves in.
We have built a home

and the ceiling is so high
everything feels about to echo—

all the things we say
growing older, and quieter, and

drifting further away.

TRANSGENDER HEROIC: ALL THIS RIDICULOUS FLESH

I.

I could say I am simple—my heart
again a newborn with a shelf life.
But there is nothing simple about
my body and its fruity orbit around
the sun. Before I had my breasts
removed from my chest, the surgeon
did not ask whether I was ready to sleep
so violently. When I woke, my nurse
made sure I felt like a woman

with a wound she didn't care
to tend. I do not regret my body
but I regret the hands of most
who have touched it. Drought loves
the dust. The desert will melt in the rain.

II.

The desert will eventually melt
in the rain. I spend so much time
worrying for the earth and its hurricane
complexion, all its cyclone acne,
that I rarely consider my own skin
and all it holds. My partner asks
me to keep my blood inside my body
and I always struggle to honor
this basic love. I tear at my skin

and at the earth, despite myself.
It is hard to remember that every
body is an ocean wave breaking.
And life is learning to labor
between our self-inflicted scars.

III.

I have made my self-inflicted scars
useful as sundials. I can tell the time
in tissue lumped hard as a dune.
When my partner and I discuss
our wedding, we choose the date
by studying the moon-scars
strapped to my chest. Sometimes,
I feel I control the water, the tide
rising when I feel most in love.

When my partner and I lift up
our lives and move, it will be toward
a lake. We will learn all the knots
that can be tied and we will tie them.
We will sail just about anywhere.

IV.

We can sail just about anywhere
in this life boat we've built
from scratch. My partner and I
have harvested the lumber
of our bones, and twined the boat-
bed with our hair. This is what
industrious lovers have mastered,
the art of floating on the flesh
of one another. I would be silly

if I said I wasn't afraid of death
when sharing a life is so sweet.
When I look at my partner's skin
I know it is as young as it will
ever be. I keep my eyes open.

v.

Young as I'll ever be, I keep my eyes
trained to my own hands and how
tenderly they hold. What happens now
will matter later and I would like
to be proud of myself and my handling
of each inherited addiction: the cough
syrup, the Klonopin, and even the malt
liquor. I've landed too many right
hooks on tree bark, too many on brick.

I am trying to change the future
my blood has written for me. And soon
I will be gentle enough to mother even
the cherry blossoms. Soon, my body will
mother whoever needs mothering most.

VI.

My body mothers just about anyone,
and I promise I can take secrets
safely through the night. I carried
my transness in a secret jeans pocket
for decades. A few times, I even
sent it through the wash, hoping
to clean what was never dirty.
I am done lying. I yearn for lost
years. I want to relive my life better.

But mostly, I wish I could tell every
trans child a story about running through
the forest shirtless, how the wind
licks when only the trees are staring.
I promise, sunrise can feel sweet.

VII.

I promise the sunrise can still feel sweet.
My partner and I keep sugar packets
in our pockets for exactly this reason.
A bit sprinkled on a halved grapefruit
and we almost forget global warming
and the ways we fail the world. Often,
when trying to ignore the pain
humans have built, I identify columns.
Doric, I say, or *Corinthian,* or *Ionic.*

Sometimes I say, *Look, Corinthian on top
and Ionic on the bottom.* My partner
reminds me that none of this matters
if the building is standing. They remind me,
being alive is the most important part.

VIII.

Just being alive is the most important
part, and on Facebook today, the baby
born premature is off oxygen, breathing
all on his own. This small joy is enough.
Imagining the cut grass he will soon smell
is enough. I have worked so hard
to feel sustained by smallness.
When it rains, the scars that rope
my chest ache like broken bones

that refuse to heal, but I am alive,
and am happy to be so. When I dream,
it is black flowers, my partner, and
the softest silences between us.
Love is the hottest summer. Let it in.

IX.

If you let it in, love can burn hotter
than summer on pavement. I've spent
winters fevering in love. I've autumned
in bandages and blood and my partner
still kissed my neck with their molten
mouth. When I was under anesthesia
my partner was not. I often imagine how
warm their hands were, wringing—
a fire started with no flint at all.

We could take this love to the forest
and live. We could feed a fire even
in a rain hell-bent on eroding bedrock.
When I sleep with my mouth open,
my partner plants mint, and it grows.

x.

My partner opens my belly and plants
rosemary. They tell me this is not
about birth, but about remembrance,
roots, and their floodwater-deep
devotion to the sea. Though my partner
will never say so, they want me to become
a cliff above an ocean, so that they might
feel safe, just once, when looking down.
I have never wanted so badly to be stable

ground until now. I would trade
my soft human skeleton for one
made exclusively of rock. I would
welcome the elements as they
hammered at the crown of my skull.

XI.

My childhood was my father's hammer
cracking down on the backs of my hands.
Don't all children with a story of abuse
know something of construction?
Tongue-and-groove pine, fitted together
in harmony, like their parents never fit.
Plywood waterlogged in a heap, untarped
and open to the rain. Who hasn't salvaged
a bent penny nail and built a fort to hide in?

We have survived on what those who
have hurt us, have taught us. What a sweet
and sour life this is. Hand me a coffee
cup of copper nails. Let me show you
how much can be built with only glue.

XII.

How much can be built with only glue?
Ask any trans person in America
what holds them together, and they
will answer: Elmer's, a few loose
stitches, and whatever love can be
harvested from Earth's sad soil.
When I am harassed on the street
I pull out my own stitches and bleed
pink, fertile waters. I feed the landscape

with my flamboyant joy. One day,
cruel people will be hungry for what
I've grown. One day, I will feed them
the fruit of their violence. And they will
feel fed. They won't yearn to hurt me at all.

XIII.

In my next life I will feel fed. I won't
hurt at all and trans people will live
just as long as everyone else.
We will build very queer sand castles
and invite everyone in. Hammocks
will hang between palm trees and all
will be well. Still an imaginative child,
I imagine this for my next body.
In America, right now, trans people

are impatient to die, because they
are hopeful for their next life.
I hope that breaks your heart.
I am angry. I am full of houseplants,
and herbs, and rage.

XIV.

I am angry. I am full of greenery
and rage. But I am still making dinner
tonight, cilantro stock boiled down—
something small to celebrate.
My partner tells me about their day,
every day. And every day I watch
their skin drink the sun's light
with an unabashed thirst for our
life together. I wish the whole

world could see the light as it floats
through our single-pane windows—could
see this particular yellow, or touch the dust
hung in time like a perfect sequined skirt.
Such simple beauty. We want to share.

xv.

My heart beat in drought until monsoon
season. All of my scars have become sails
that can be used to sail anywhere. And
now, young as I'll ever be, I keep my body
ready to mother those who most need it.
I promise the next sunrise will feel sweet.
Just being alive is the most important part,
and since I've let it, love has burnt open
my belly and planted the greenest crops.

Though I've only known the hammer,
I will build so much with glue. Watch me
build a life and feel fed. I'll leave hurt
at the door. I am so painfully full of love.
I could even say my heart is simple, again.

ACKNOWLEDGMENTS

Endless gratitude to editors of the following publications for publishing many of the poems in this collection, often in different forms.

Academy of American Poets Poem-a-Day: "One geography of belonging"

The American Poetry Review: "You've heard this before: the only way out is through"

Crab Orchard Review: "On the ways our mouths betray us"

Foundry: "On traveling together" and "Water I won't touch" (My partner & I only believe)

Fourteen Hills: "Water we won't touch"

Gulf Coast: "We remain foolishly hopeful (or, obituary for the topsoil)"

The Journal: "On the abuse of sleep aids" and "Summering in Wildwood, NJ"

The Normal School: "Transgender heroic: all this ridiculous flesh"

The Offing: "Sand & silt"

Peach Mag: "Some thoughts on luck"

Poetry: "My partner wants me to write them a poem about Sheryl Crow" and "Sestina written as though genesis"

Portland Review: "On crescents & waning"

Puerto del Sol: "On having forgotten to recycle"

Territory: "Valentine, Nebraska: Cherry County"

TIMBER: "Echo"

TriQuarterly: "Here we are, aging together, just like we said we would"

Washington Square Review: "My partner wants me to write them a poem about Drew Barrymore"

Yalobusha Review: "On the benefits of learning by example"

LIGHTS & LOVES

Endless gratitude to the entire Copper Canyon team, who made this dream come true.

Gratitude beyond words to the Whiting Foundation and to the National Endowment for the Arts.

So many thanks to Michael Martone, Wendy Rawlings, and L. Lamar Wilson, who never quit on me. Thank you to Eduardo Corral, Geffrey Davis, and T Kira Madden for spending time and energy with these poems.

A special shout-out to Manny Brown's and Harry's Smoke Shop in Philadelphia, PA. It's a true gift to write poems while surrounded by friends.

And to my perfect friends—who endure so many EDM mix CDs—please know I'm yours through any storm. Light-years of love to: Alexis Hunte, Amy Horrigan, Anna Ladd, Aqua Dublavee, Berry Grass, Brian Oliu, Carli Fiorentini, Chelsea Leese, Cody Hohl, C. Russell Price, Danielle Gartner, Despy Boutris, Diamond Forde, Eric Schaeffer, Erik Kline, Ever Sugarman, Geoffrey Emerson, Grant TerBush, Hannah Rubin, Jenifer Park, Joshua Sanders, Julia Coursey, Kit Emslie, Laura Kochman, Laura Miller, Lauren Alvarez, Lauren DeLucca, Lauren Hilger, Lindsay Woodack, Maggie Sipps, Marina Oney, Marlon Salazar, Megan Murray, MK Foster, Nabila Lovelace, Rachel Brown, Rachel Dispenza, RBrown, Reem Abu-Baker, Remy Montgomery-Rodgers, Sam Malandra-Myers, Shaelyn Smith, Shaina Nasrin, shelley feller, and all my other glowstick & glitter-loving buddies.

Oceans of thanks to Momma Bear, Grandmommy, Nana, Kimmy, Tom, Keri, Lila, Chrissy, Tor, and Blue. Y'all keep me afloat.

Rivers and roads of love and thanks to Jackie Papanier. Because of you, every window is open, every breeze is gentle, and all the lights, of course, are floating.

ABOUT THE AUTHOR

Kayleb Rae Candrilli is the recipient of a Whiting Award and of a fellowship from the National Endowment for the Arts. They are the author of *Water I Won't Touch*, *All the Gay Saints* (Saturnalia, 2020), and *What Runs Over* (YesYes Books, 2017). *All the Gay Saints* won the 2019 Saturnalia book contest. *What Runs Over* won the 2016 Pamet River Prize and was a finalist for the Lambda Literary Award in transgender poetry.

Candrilli earned an MA in Creative Writing from Pennsylvania State University, and they hold both an MFA and an MLIS degree from the University of Alabama. Their work is published in *Poetry*, *The American Poetry Review*, *TriQuarterly*, *Boston Review*, and many others. Candrilli lives in Philadelphia with their partner.

Poetry is vital to language and living. Since 1972, Copper Canyon Press has published extraordinary poetry from around the world to engage the imaginations and intellects of readers, writers, booksellers, librarians, teachers, students, and donors.

Copper Canyon Press gratefully acknowledges the kindness, patronage, and generous support of Jean Marie Lee, whose love and passionate appreciation of poetry has provided an everlasting benefit to our publishing program.

WE ARE GRATEFUL FOR THE MAJOR SUPPORT PROVIDED BY:

THE PAUL G. ALLEN
FAMILY FOUNDATION

CULTURE

Lannan

OFFICE OF ARTS & CULTURE
SEATTLE

WASHINGTON STATE
ARTS COMMISSION